John Lawson Stoddard

China

John Lawson Stoddard

China

ISBN/EAN: 9783337164355

Printed in Europe, USA, Canada, Australia, Japan

Cover: Foto ©Andreas Hilbeck / pixelio.de

More available books at **www.hansebooks.com**

CHINA

BY

JOHN L. STODDARD

ILLUSTRATED AND EMBELLISHED WITH ONE HUNDRED
AND TWENTY-TWO REPRODUCTIONS OF
PHOTOGRAPHS

CHICAGO
BELFORD, MIDDLEBROOK & COMPANY
MDCCCXCVII

ENTERED AT STATIONERS' HALL, LONDON
ALL RIGHTS RESERVED

CHINA

CHINA defies the world to equal her in three important respects: age, population, and industries. As for the first, she undoubtedly has the oldest Government on earth. Even the Papacy is young compared with it; and as for our republic, it is a thing of yesterday. A Chinaman once said to an American: "Wait till your Government has been tried before you boast of it. What is a hundred years? Ours has stood the test of forty centuries. When you did not exist, we were. When you shall have passed away, we still shall be."

In point of numbers, too, the Chinese empire leads the world. Its area is nearly twice as large as that of the United States, and it has six times as many people. The governor of one Chinese province rules over sixty million souls. Have we a definite conception of what four hundred million human beings are? Arrange the inhabitants of our globe in one long line, and every fourth man will be a Chinaman.

EMPEROR OF CHINA.

As for her industries, Musa, the Saracen conqueror of Spain, once aptly said that Wisdom, when she came from heaven to earth, was lodged in the head of the Greeks, the tongue of the Arabs, and the hands of the Chinese. China was once what the United States is now—the birthplace of inventions. Paper was manufactured there in the third century of our era. Tea was produced a century later. If Europe had enjoyed communication with China, it would

A CHINESE TEMPLE.

have learned the art of printing many centuries before it did; and who can say what might have been the result? A thousand years ago the Chinese made designs on wood. Printing from stone was a still earlier industry among them. In China, also, gunpowder was first invented—a thought by which, alas! so many thoughts have been destroyed. This same astonishing race produced the mariner's compass in the fourth century, porcelain in the third, chess and playing-cards in the twelfth, and silk embroideries in almost prehistoric times. An empire, therefore, of such vast antiquity, overwhelming population, and great achievements must be, despite its faults, a country of absorbing interest.

The most delightful portion of the voyage from Japan to China lies in the Japanese Mediterranean, known as the Inland Sea. It is a miniature ocean, practically land-locked for three hundred miles, with both shores constantly in sight, yet strewn with islands of all shapes and sizes, from small and uninhabited rocks to wave-encircled hills, terraced and cultivated to their very summits. It seems as if volcanic action here had caused the land to sink, until the ocean rushed in and submerged it, leaving only the highest peaks above the waves.

We lingered here all day upon the steamer's deck, like passengers on the Rhine, fearing to lose a single feature of the varied panorama gliding by on either side. By night it was more glorious even than by day; for then, from every danger-

THE JAPANESE MEDITERRANEAN.

ous cliff flashed forth a beacon light; the villages along the shore displayed a line of glittering points, like constellations rising from the sea; and, best of all, at a later hour, moonlight lent enchantment to the scene, drawing a crystal edge

WAVE-ENCIRCLED HILLS.

along each mountain crest, and making every island seem a jewel on a silver thread.

When we emerged from these inland waters, we saw between us and the setting sun the stretch of ocean called the China Sea. At certain seasons of the year this is the favorite pathway of typhoons; and the Formosa Channel, in particular, has been a graveyard for countless vessels. Indeed, only three weeks before, a sister

HUGE SAILS LIKE THE WINGS OF BATS.

ship of ours—the "Bokhara,"—had gone down here in a terrific cyclone. Yet when we sailed its waters nothing could have been more beautiful. Day after day this sea of evil omen rested motionless, like a sleek tigress gorged with food and basking in the sun.

After a three-days' voyage from the Japanese coast, we began to meet, in constantly increasing numbers, large, pointed boats, propelled by huge sails ribbed with cross-bars, like the wings of bats. Upon the bow of each was painted an

THE HARBOR OF HONG-KONG.

enormous eye; for of their sailing craft the mariners of China, in elementary English, say: "If boat no have eye, how can boat see go?" We were assured that these were Chinese sailing craft, and that our destination was not far away; but it was difficult to realize this, and I remember looking off beyond those ships and trying to convince myself that we were actually on the opposite side of the globe from home and friends, and in a few brief hours were to land in that vast Eastern empire so full of mystery in its exclusiveness, antiquity, and changeless calm.

That night the agitation that precedes one's first arrival in a foreign land made sleep almost impossible. It seemed to me that I had not closed my eyes when suddenly the steamer stopped. To my astonishment, the morning light had already found its way into my state-room. We had arrived! Hurrying to the deck, therefore, I looked upon the glorious harbor of Hong-Kong. A hundred ships and steamers lay at anchor here, displaying flags of every country on the globe. Although the day had hardly dawned, these waters

THE CITY OF VICTORIA.

showed great animation. Steam-launches, covered with white awnings, were darting to and fro like flying-fish. Innumerable smaller boats, called *sampans*, propelled by Chinese men and women, surrounded each incoming steamer, like porpoises around a whale. On one side rose some barren-looking mountains, which were a part of the mainland of China; but for the moment they presented little to attract us. It was the other shore of this magnificent harbor that awoke our interest; for there we saw an island twenty-seven miles in circumference, covered with mountains rising boldly from the sea.

THE PUBLIC GARDENS.

Along the base of one of these elevations, and built in terraces far up on its precipitous slopes, was a handsome city.

"What is this?" we inquired eagerly.

"The town itself," was the reply, "is called Victoria, but this imposing island to whose flank it clings, is, as you may suppose, Hong-Kong."

The first impression made upon me here was that of mild astonishment at the architecture. Almost without exception, the prominent buildings of Victoria have on every story deep porticoes divided by columns into large, square spaces, which

A STREET IN HONG-KONG.

from a distance look like letter-boxes in a post-office. We soon discovered that such deep, shadowy verandas are essential here, for as late as November it was imprudent not to carry a white umbrella, and even before our boat had brought us from the steamer to the pier, we perceived that the solar rays were not to be trifled with.

As soon as possible after landing, we started to explore this British settlement. I was delighted with its streets and buildings. The former are broad, smooth and clean; the latter, three or four stories high, are built of granite, and even on a curve have sidewalks shielded from the sun or rain by the projection of the roof above. Truly, the touch of England has wrought astounding changes in the fifty-five years that she has held this island as her own. Before she came it was the resort of poverty-stricken fishermen and pirates.

DEEP PORTICOES AND COLONNADES.

But now the city of Victoria alone contains two hundred thousand souls, while the grand aqueducts and roads which cross the mountains of Hong-Kong are worthy to be compared with some of the monumental works of ancient Rome.

Along the principal thoroughfare in Victoria, the banks, shops, hotels, and club-houses, which succeed each other rapidly, are built of the fine gray granite of the adjacent mountains, and show handsome architectural designs. Everything looks as trim and spotless as the appointments of a man-of-war. Even the district of the town inhabited by Chinamen is kept by constant watchfulness immeasurably cleaner than a Chinese city; although if one desires to see the world-wide difference that exists between the British and Mongolian races, he merely needs to take a short walk through the Chinese quarter of Victoria. But such comparisons may well be deferred until one reaches Canton. There one beholds the genuine native article.

The police who guard the lives and property of the residents of Hong-Kong, are for the most part picked men of English birth, and are considered as trustworthy as regular troops. But several hundred of these guardians of the peace are Sikhs—a race imported hither from India—renowned for bravery, loyal to the British government, and having no sympathy with the Chinese. These Sikhs have handsome faces, brilliant eyes, and dark complexions, the effect of which is wonderfully enhanced by their immense red turbans, con-

THE BANK, HONG-KONG.

spicuous two or three blocks away, not only by their startling color, but because their wearers exceed in stature all other races in Hong-Kong.

Strolling one morning through the outskirts of the city, I came upon some troops engaged in military manœuvres, and attired in white from head to foot, to shield them from the sun. What traveler in the East can forget the ever-present soldiers of Great Britain, of whom there are nearly three

POLICEMEN.

thousand in the garrison of Hong-Kong? I know it is frequently the fashion to sneer at them and to question their efficiency in case of war. I know, too, that in certain ways the vast extent of England's empire constitutes her weakness. But I must say that in a tour around our planet I was impressed as never before with what the British had accomplished in the way of conquest, and with the number of strategic points they hold in every quarter of the globe. We had but recently left the western terminus of England's North American possessions, yet in a few days we discerned the flag of England flying at Hong-Kong. Next we beheld the Union Jack at Singapore, then at Penang, then

SOLDIERS DRILLING.

at Ceylon, and after that throughout the length and breadth of the vast empire of India, as well as the enormous area of Burma. Leaving Rangoon, if we sail southward, we are

CHINESE COBBLER.

reminded that the southernmost portion of Africa is entirely in English hands, as well as the huge continent of Australia. Returning northward, we find the same great colonizing power stationed at the mouth of the Red Sea, in the British

A BIT OF CHINATOWN IN HONG-KONG.

citadel of Aden. Again a trifling journey, and we reach Egypt, *via* the Suez Canal, both virtually controlled to-day by England. Then, like the three stars in Orion's belt, across the Mediterranean lie Cyprus, Malta, and Gibraltar; in fact, we find one mighty girdle of imposing strongholds all the way, bristling with cannon, guarded by leviathans in armor, and garrisoned by thousands of such soldiers as were drilling at Hong-Kong.

One of the first desires of the visitor to Hong-Kong is to explore the mountain which towers above the city of Victoria to a height of nearly two thousand feet. To do this with the least exertion, each of our party took a canvas-covered bamboo chair, supported by long poles, which Chinese coolies carry on their shoulders. On level ground, two of these bearers were enough, but on the mountain roads three or

CHAIR-COOLIES AT HONG-KONG.

four men were usually needed. To my surprise, I found the motion of these chairs agreeable. The poles possess such elasticity that, leaning back, I was rocked lightly up and down without the least unpleasant jar. In fact, at times the rhythm of that oscillation gave me a sense of drowsiness difficult to resist.

But, alas! we had not here for carriers the cleanly natives of Japan. It may be, as some residents of Hong-Kong assert, that Chinamen are more trustworthy and honest than the Japanese, but certainly in point of personal attractiveness the contrast between these races is remarkable. The bodies of the lower classes of Chinese reveal no evidence of that care so characteristic of the natives of Japan. Their teeth are often yellow tusks; their nails resemble eagle's claws; and their unbecoming clothes seem glazed by perspiration. Nor is there usually anything in their manner to redeem all this. Where the light-hearted Japs enjoy their work, and laugh and talk, the Chinese coolies labor painfully, and rarely smile.

THE MOUNTAIN ABOVE VICTORIA.

regarding you meantime with a supercilious air, as if despising you for being what they call "a foreign devil."

Nevertheless, despite the repulsive appearance of our bearers, we thoroughly enjoyed our excursion up the mountain. At every step our admiration was increased for the magnificent roads which wind about the cliffs in massive terraces, arched over by majestic trees, bordered by parapets of stone, lighted with gas, and lined with broad, deep aqueducts, through which at times the copious rainfall rushes like a mountain stream. It will be seen that such a comparison is not an exaggeration, when I add that not many years ago, thirty-two inches of rain fell here in thirty hours. This mountain is the favorite abode of wealthy foreigners, and hence these curving avenues present on either side, almost to

THE CABLE-ROAD TO VICTORIA PEAK.

the summit, a series of attractive villas commanding lovely views. On account of their situation, the gardens of these hillside homes are necessarily small; but in the midst of them, about five hundred feet above the town, a charming botanical park has been laid out.

Forgetful of our coolies at the gate, we lingered in this garden for an hour or two, delighted with its fine display of semitropical foliage. It is marvelous what skillful gardeners have accomplished here, in transforming what was fifty years ago a barren rock into an open-air conservatory. Palms, banyans, india-rubber trees, mimosas with their tufts of gold, camellias with their snowy blossoms—all these are here, with roses, mignonette, and jessamine, surrounded with innumerable ferns. Occasionally we encountered in this fragrant area a Chinese gentleman, indulging leisurely his love of flowers; for this delightful park is open to all without regard to race or creed, although the population of the island is extremely cosmopolitan. Englishmen, Americans, Germans, Frenchmen, Spaniards, Portuguese, Italians, Parsees, Mohammedans, Jews, Hindus, and fully one hundred and fifty thousand Chinamen, are residents of the city of Victoria alone.

In this retired park one does not realize that Hong-Kong is such a rendezvous for different nationalities; but frequently, while we were walking here, the sharp report of a cannon forced a discordant echo from the neighboring hills and told us that some foreign man-of-war had just appeared within the bay; for here some ship or steamer is continually arriving or departing, and many times a day there comes a deafening interchange of salutes that sends a thrill through every window-pane upon the mountain.

THE BOTANICAL PARK, HONG-KONG.

One can well understand, therefore, that with so mixed a population and in such close proximity to China, the officers sent out here by the British government must be men of courage, the garrison of the island strong, and its administration prompt and resolute. A single incident revealed to me the crimes which would undoubtedly creep forth, like vipers from a loathsome cave, were they not kept in check by vigorous justice and incessant vigilance.

In one of the residences on the height above Victoria, I met one day at dinner the captain of a steamer anchored in the bay. He asked me to come out some evening and pay a

AN OPEN-AIR CONSERVATORY.

visit to his ship. The following night, soon after dark, I walked down to the pier, intending to embark on one of the many boats along the shore. I was about to enter one, when a policeman rapidly approached. "Give me your name and number," he said roughly to the Chinese boatman. Then turning to me, he politely asked my name, address, and destination, and when I intended to return. "I am obliged to do this," he explained, "for your protection. There is a population of twenty thousand Chinese living in this harbor

A HONG-KONG STREET—IN THE CHINESE QUARTER.

IN THE BUSINESS SECTION, HONG-KONG.

upon boats alone, besides the usual criminals who drift to such a place. Before we adopted this precaution, a foreigner would sometimes embark on one of these craft and never be seen again. In such a case search was useless. He had disappeared as quietly and thoroughly as a piece of silver dropped into the bay."

When I stood on the apex of Victoria Peak, I thought that I had never seen a finer prospect. Nearly two thou-

VIEW FROM
VICTORIA PEAK.

sand feet below us lay the renowned metropolis of the East
which bears the name of England's queen. From this great
elevation, its miles of granite blocks resembled a stupendous
landslide, which, sweeping downward from this rocky height,
had forced its cracked and creviced mass far out into the bay.
Between this and the mainland opposite, curved a portion of
that ocean-girdle which surrounds the island, and on its surface countless boats and steamers seemed, in the long perspective, like ornaments of bead-work on a lady's belt.

Around the summit of the mountain are several handsome
villas and hotels, whither the residents of Victoria come in
summer to escape the heat; but, as a rule, in riding over the
island I saw outside of the city very few houses, and little
agriculture. The soil of Hong-Kong is not fer-
tile; but politically and commercially the island
is immensely valuable, for England has now made
of it the great emporium of the Far East, and, garrisoned by British troops, it guards completely the
approaches to that river, upon which, ninety-two
miles inland from the ocean, lies the city of
Canton.

THE RACE-TRACK, HONG-KONG.

One of the pleasantest
excursions in Hong-Kong
may be made in sedan-chairs, some six miles over the hills, to
the great reservoir which supplies the city with water. The
aqueduct which comes from it is solidly constructed, and on its
summit is a granite path protected by iron railings. This

winds along the cliffs for miles, and is in many places cut through solid rock. It is an illustration of the handsome, yet substantial character of everything accomplished here. One feels that such works are not only artistic, but enduring. Here

THE AQUEDUCT, HONG-KONG.

are no wooden trestles, no hastily constructed bridges and no half-made roads to be destroyed by mountain torrents, but everywhere the best of masonry, cyclopean in massiveness and perfect in detail.

On reaching the terminus of this granite pathway we saw before us the principal reservoir of Hong-Kong. Though largely artificial, it looks precisely like a natural lake hidden away among the mountains. Before it was constructed the island's water-supply was lamentably insufficient, and the notorious "Hong-Kong fever" gave the place an evil name. But now, in spite of its large native population, Victoria has as low a death-rate as most European cities. The foreign residents are very proud of these magnificent water-works; yet, after ten days' sojourn here, when I took leave of several gentlemen by whom I had been entertained in private houses and at clubs, candor compelled me to confess that, so far as I had been able to observe, the foreign population makes very little use of this water for drinking purposes.

A MOUNTAIN ROAD, HONG-KONG.

On starting to descend the mountain, we found a shorter route than the circuitous path by which we had come — an admirably managed cable-road. In viewing this, the question naturally arises how the Chinese can look on such conveniences as England has here introduced, and still remain content to have in their enormous empire scarcely a decent road, and only a few miles of railway, built to transport coal. Canals

AN EASY DESCENT.

A CHINESE ROAD.

and rivers are still the usual arteries of travel through the most of China. In the northern provinces, where carts are used, the roads are often worn below the surface of the adjacent land, and hence become, in the rainy season, mere water-courses. Travelers are occasionally obliged to swim across them; and cases have been known of people drowning in a Chinese roadway. Moreover, the characteristic carts of China are of the most primitive description, having no seats except the floor, and no springs save the involuntary ones contributed by their luckless passengers. Yet, in many districts, even such vehicles can find no path, and people travel about in wheelbarrows propelled by coolies

A CHINESE VEHICLE.

who are sometimes aided by a sail. The Bishop of North China, for example, makes many of his parochial visits in a wheelbarrow.

There is now in China a small progressive party which favors building railroads, as the Japanese have done, but the immense majority are against it. Some years ago a foreign company built a railroad near Shanghai, but the Chinese speedily bought it up at a great cost, transported the rails and

CHINESE GRAVES.

locomotives to the sea, and left them to rust upon the beach This opposition to railways is principally due to the belief that the use of them would deprive millions of people of their means of gaining a livelihood, and that they would, moreover, disturb the graveyards of the country. This latter objection seems at first incredible; but it must be remembered that Chinese cemeteries are strewn broadcast over the land.

> "Thick as autumnal leaves that strow the brooks
> In Vallombrosa."

One sees them everywhere, usurping valuable tracts of territory needed for the living. Outside the city of Canton, for

HONG KONG.

example, there is a graveyard thirty miles in length, in which are buried fully one hundred generations. Yet the Chinese insist that not one grave shall be disturbed, lest multitudes of avenging ghosts

AN ELABORATE TOMB.

should be let loose upon them for such sacrilege. In fact, the permanence and inviolability of graves lie at the very foundation of Chinese life and customs, which is ancestor-worship. From childhood to old age the principal duty of all Chinamen is to propitiate the spirits of their ances-

THE FOREIGN CEMETERY, HONG-KONG.

A FELLOW PASSENGER.

tors, and to make offerings to them regularly at their tombs. This custom cripples the colossal empire of China as paralysis would a giant, and fear of doing violence to their dead holds China's millions in an iron grasp.

The discussion of this theme, as we were descending the mountain, suggested to us the idea of visiting the foreign cemetery in Hong-Kong. In this, as in the public garden, charming results have been obtained by care and irrigation. We were accompanied by a gentleman who had resided on the island nearly thirty years. "In spite of the beauty of this place," he said, "I dread to think that I shall probably be buried here—unable to escape from China even after death. For notwithstanding many pleasant friends, my life, like that of many here, has been at best a dreary banishment from all that makes your Occidental life so stimulating to the intellect

ON THE CANTON RIVER.

and so rich in pleasures. The world at home," he added, "sometimes blames us for faults, the cause of which is often only an intense desire to counteract the loneliness of our existence; and foreigners in the East deserve some sympathy, if only from the fact that in these cemeteries, kept with so much care, the graves of those we love increase so rapidly."

After a few days at Hong-Kong we embarked on one of the American steamers which ply between Victoria and Canton. These boats are modest imitations of the Fall River steamers on Long Island Sound. We found the one that we

RIVER BOATS.

took clean and comfortable and its American captain cordial and communicative. During the trip he related to us many incidents of his life in China. This he could easily do, for there were only two other foreign passengers on board, and hence, so long as we remained upon the promenade deck, the spacious vessel seemed to be our private yacht.

On passing, however, to the deck below, we found a number of Chinamen, likewise going to Canton. Most of them were smoking, lying on their backs, their heads supported by a bale of cloth. At first we thought these constituted all the passengers; but presently we learned, to our astonishment, that farther down, packed in the hold like sardines in a box, and barricaded from us by an iron grating, were more than a thousand Chinese coolies. A sentry, heavily armed, stood by the padlocked grating constantly; while in the wheel-house and saloon were stands of loaded

EXECUTION OF THE PIRATES.

muskets ready for emergencies. The danger is that Chinese pirates will come on board in the disguise of coolies, and at a favorable moment take possession of the ship. One naturally thinks this an impossible occurrence; but only a few years ago this actually took place on one of these boats. A well-armed band of desperadoes swarmed up from the hold, shot down the captain in cold blood, and also some of the passengers who tried to interfere. Then, taking command of the ship, they forced the engineer and crew to do their bidding, steered to a lonely point where their confederates awaited them, unloaded the valuable cargo into their boats, disabled the engine so that the survivors could not give the alarm, and finally made their escape. Such are the indisputable facts. Yet, sailing up this peaceful river, reclining in our easy chairs, and soothed by the soft, balmy air, the tragedy seemed so incredible that we were obliged to put our hands upon the guns, in order to realize that precautions were still needed.

As an additional proof, the captain showed us a photograph of the sequel to that act of piracy. For, as a matter of course, the British Government demanded satisfaction for this outrage, and in compliance nineteen criminals were beheaded. Whether they were the actual pirates, however, has been doubted. China always has scores of men awaiting execution—a dozen here, a dozen there. What matters it if those who merit death are said to have committed one crime or another? England had no way of identifying them. Accordingly she shut her eyes, accepted what the Chinese said of them, and took it for granted that the decapitated men were the real culprits. At all events, as an eye-witness told us, the deed itself was quickly done. In each case there was

WITH STARING EYES TURNED UPWARD.

only one swing of the executioner's arm, and one flash of the two-edged sword; then, like a row of flowers clipped from their stems, the heads of all the kneeling criminals were lying in the sand, with staring eyes turned upward toward the sky.

On leaving this repulsive picture in the captain's cabin, we found that we were approaching the once important settlement of Whampoa. Its glory is gone now,

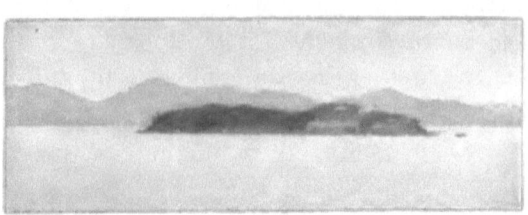

AN OLD CHINESE FORT, CANTON RIVER.

OPIUM-SMOKING.

but formerly it played a prominent part in Eastern politics and commerce; for previous to the Opium War of 1841 and the establishment of the Treaty Ports, this was as far as foreign ships were permitted to come, and Whampoa was then a kind of counter across which Cantonese and Europeans traded. We now began to observe along the shore strange-looking boats protected by a roof and filled with fruits and vegetables for the Canton market. Moreover, on

SINGING GIRLS.

both sides of the river for many miles we looked on countless little patches of rice, bananas, oranges, and sugar-cane. At one point our attention was called to an island on which are some old fortifications used by China fifty years ago in her attempt to exclude opium from her territory. I suppose that no intelligent student of the subject doubts that the real cause of the war of 1841 was the attempt of England to force upon the Chinese a drug which no one dares to sell in London, even now, unless it bears the label "poison." In 1840, the Commissioner of Canton thus addressed the Queen of England:

"How can your country seek to acquire wealth by selling us an article so injurious to mankind? I have heard that you have a gen-

A CHINESE BRIDGE.

erous heart; you must be willing, therefore, to obey the motto of Confucius, and refuse to do to others what you would not have others do to you."

In an address to foreign traders, issued in 1840, the Chinese also said: "Reflect that if you did not bring opium here, where could our people obtain it? Shall, then, our people die, and your lives not be required? You are destroying human life for the sake of gain. You should surrender your opium out of regard for the natural feelings of mankind. If not, it is right for us to drive every ship of your nation from our shores."

Finding that these appeals were of no avail, the Chinese finally compelled the British merchants in Canton to give up all the opium in their possession. It amounted to twenty-one thousand chests, or about three million pounds. This

THE CURSE OF CHINA.

mass of poison the Chinese threw into the river, chest after chest, much as Americans treated English tea in Boston harbor. As it dissolved, it is said that a large number of fish died. England retaliated by broadsides from her men-of-war, and in 1842, after an unequal struggle, China was forced to pay her victorious enemy twenty-one million dollars —six millions for the opium destroyed, and fifteen millions as a war indemnity, besides giving to England as her property forever, the island of Hong-Kong, and opening five new ports to foreign trade.

About a century ago opium was rarely used in China except as medicine. To-day it enters through the openings made by English cannon, at the rate of six thousand tons a year, and at an annual profit to the Indian treasury of from thirty to forty million dollars. But this is not the worst: the vice of opium-smoking has spread with such rapidity that in one Chinese city alone, where thirty years ago only five opium dens existed, there are now five thousand. In the minds of many Chinamen, therefore, Christianity is principally associated with the gift of opium and its attendant evils. China has now begun to cultivate the poppy for herself, and in some provinces six-tenths of the land is given over to producing opium, to the great detriment of agriculture. For the Chinese argue that if they must have it anyway, they may as well profit by it themselves, and let their own crop vie with that which England sends from India. It should be said that earnest protests have often been made by conscientious Englishmen against this conduct of their Government, but all

A VILLAGE SCENE.

remonstrances have failed to change its policy. Hence, when our British cousins sometimes humorously say that we Americans worship only the almighty dollar, it may be well to ask if any deity under the sun is more devoutly reverenced than the omnipotent pounds, shillings, and pence.

When we had steamed about five hours from Hong-Kong, we came in sight of our first Chinese pagoda. It is a hollow tower of brick about three hundred feet in height, and resembles, on an enormous scale, one of those tapering sticks which jewelers use for sizing rings. At first, I thought that the nine circular terraces which mark its different stories were adorned with flags or tapestry, but closer scrutiny revealed the melancholy fact that weeds and bushes are now growing here. Indeed, like most of the sacred buildings that I saw in China, it looked both dirty and dilapidated.

Soon after leaving this neglected edifice, we found ourselves amid a constantly increasing throng of Chinese boats, and I began to realize that these were specimens of that "floating population" of Canton of which we have all read, but of which nothing but a visit to it can give an adequate idea.

PAGODA, NEAR CANTON RIVER.

Hardly was our steamer anchored in the stream before the city, when hundreds of these boats closed in upon us on all sides, like cakes of floating ice around a vessel in the Arctic sea. Wedging and pushing frantically, the boatmen almost swamped themselves. They fought for places near the ship like men and women in a panic. The din of voices sounded like the barking of five hundred canines at a dog-show; and Chinese gutturals flew through the air like bullets from a *mitrailleuse*. It seemed impossible to disembark in such a mob.

But suddenly I felt a pressure on my arm. I turned and saw apparently three laundrymen from the United States.

A glance assured me they were father and sons. "Good morning, sir," said one of them in excellent English, "do you know Carter Harrison, of Chicago?"

This question, coming in such a place and at such a time, rendered me speechless with astonishment.

NEARING CANTON.

"He mentioned us in his book, 'A Race with the Sun,'" continued the young Chinaman. "This is my father, the famous guide, Ah Cum. This is my brother, and I am Ah Cum, Jr. The others are engaged for to-morrow, but I can serve you. Will you take me?"

"So you are Ah Cum?" I rejoined; "I have heard much of you. Your reference book must be a valuable autograph album of distinguished travelers. Yes, we will take you; and, first of all, can you get us safely into one of those boats? And if so, who will guarantee that we shall not be murdered?"

"Ah Cum."

Accordingly we "came," and presently found ourselves in a boat. I cannot relate how we got there. I do not know, myself. I think of it now as one recalls the pulling of a tooth when under the influence of laughing-gas. I have a dim remembrance of jumping from one reeling skiff to another, of stumbling over slippery seats, of holding on to Ah Cum, Sr., and being pushed by Ah Cum, Jr., and now and then grabbing frantically at a Chinese queue, as a drowning man catches at a rope. The only reason that I did not fall into the water is that there was not space enough between the boats. At last, however, bruised and breathless, we reached a place of refuge, and watched our boatmen fight their way out through the crowd, until we landed on the neighboring island of Shameen. After the pandemonium around the steamer, this seemed a perfect paradise of beauty and repose. It is about a mile and a quarter in circumference, and is reserved exclusively for foreigners.

CHINESE BOATS, CANTON.

Shaded by drooping banyan trees, stand many handsome houses inhabited by Englishmen, Germans, and Americans whom the necessities of business keep in banishment here. Their social life is said to be very pleasant, and I should think, indeed, that in so small a settlement the members of this little colony (if they did not hate) would love each other cordially. This pretty place, before the capture of Canton, in 1857, was nothing but a hideous mud-bank. But foreigners have transformed it almost as completely as they have Hong-Kong, and have built around it broad

THE FLOATING HOMES OF THOUSANDS, CANTON.

embankments made of solid granite, which form an agreeable promenade.

Unfortunately, however, Shameen boasts of only one hotel, and of this such dismal stories had been told us that we had half made up our minds to eat and sleep on the American steamers, changing from one to another every morning as they

INTERIOR OF A EUROPEAN'S HOUSE.

came and went. This seemed, however, so difficult, that we resolved to try the accommodations here. We did so, and discovered that in this case "the devil is not so black as he is painted." At all events, clean, comfortable rooms made some amends for a meager bill of fare.

I cherish no delightful recollections of our meals on the island of Shameen. In fact, when a "globe-trotter" has reached India or China, the time has come for him to eat what he can get, and be devoutly thankful that he can get anything. Misguided souls who live to eat should never make a journey around the world. Of course, the foreign residents here live better than travelers at hotels; but a gentleman who entertained us apologized for his poor table, and said that it was especially difficult to get good beef, since Chinamen consider it extravagant to kill such useful animals as cows and oxen. "Accordingly," he added, "we classify the so-called beef that we consume as 'donkey beef,' 'camel beef,' and 'precipice beef.'"

THE JINRIKISHA IN CHINA.

"Precipice beef!" I exclaimed. "what in the world do you mean by 'precipice beef?'"

"That," he replied, "is nearest to the genuine article, for it is the product of a cow that has killed herself by falling over a precipice."

On one side of this island flows the Canton river, and on the other is a small canal which separates it from the city. Two bridges span this narrow stream, each having iron gates which are invariably closed at night and guarded by sentinels. No Chinese, save employees of the foreigners, may come within this reservation. In 1883, however, a Chinese mob attacked it fiercely, and swarmed across the bridges, as the legendary mice invaded Bishop Hatto's tower on the Rhine. The English, French, and German families escaped

STARTING FOR CANTON.

to steamers in the river, leaving their houses to be plundered or burned. During my stay here, every evening when this bridge was closed, and every morning when it was reopened, I heard a hideous din of drums and horns, concluding with the firing of a blunderbuss. Our consul told me that the object of all this was to inspire fear. "Tremble and obey!" are the words which close all Government proclamations in the Chinese empire.

The morning after our arrival, we found awaiting us outside the hotel door some coolies with the sedan-chairs in

BRIDGE AT CANTON.

which we were to make our first excursion through Canton. Another party also was about to start, including several ladies, each of whom held in her hand either a flask of smelling-salts or a piece of camphor wrapped in a handkerchief. In fact, the druggists of Hong-Kong do quite a business in furnishing visitors to Canton with disinfectants and restoratives. Some of these ladies feared being insulted by the Canton populace, and told exciting stories of an English lady who had been recently spat upon, and of American ladies who had been followed by a hooting crowd. Ah Cum, however, smiled complacently.

A CANTON STREET.

"There is no danger," he assured us; "my father will take care of you ladies, as I will of these gentlemen. Every one here knows us. *Our* people are always safe."

Accordingly we started, crossed the bridge, and two minutes later found ourselves engulfed, like atoms in a sewer, in the fetid labyrinth of Canton. One should not be surprised that illustrations of its streets are not clearer. The marvel is that they are visible at all! "Streets," as we understand the word, they cannot be truthfully called. They are dark,

ALONG THE SHORE, CANTON

tortuous alleys, destitute of sidewalks, and from four to eight feet wide, winding snake-like between long lines of gloomy shops. Comparatively little daylight filters through them to the pavement, not only by reason of their narrow limits, but from the fact that all these passageways are largely filled up, just above the people's heads, with strips of wood, which serve as advertising placards. Many of them are colored blue, red, white, or green, and bear strange characters, gilded or painted on their surfaces. These in the dark perspective of a crowded alley look like the banners of some long procession.

These letters do not give the merchants' names, but serve as trade-marks, like the dedicatory words

TEMPLE OF CONFUCIUS, CANTON.

above the doors of shops in France. How any one can read them is a mystery; not merely on account of the twilight gloom, but from the fact that here at every step one comes in contact with a multitude of repulsive Chinamen, many of them naked to the waist, who seem compressed within this narrow space like a wild torrent in a gorge. To stop in such a place and read a sign appeared to me as difficult as studying the leaves of the trees while riding through a forest on a Texas broncho.

As our bearers pushed their way through these dark,

narrow lanes, the people squeezed themselves against the walls to let us pass; then closed about us instantly again, like sharks around the stern of a boat. At any moment I could have touched a dozen naked shoulders with my hand, and twice as many with my cane. Meanwhile, to the noise of the loquacious multitude were added the vociferations of our bearers, who shouted constantly for people to make way, ascribing to us, we were told, distinguished titles that evidently excited curiosity even among the stolid Chinamen. Occasionally we met a sedan-chair coming in the opposite direction. Both sets of bearers then began to yell like maniacs, and we would finally pass each other with the utmost difficulty, our coolies having frequently to back the chair-poles into one shop, and then run them forward into a doorway on the opposite corner, thereby blocking the noisy, surly crowd until the passage could be cleared.

A CANTON COOLIE.

The faces packed about us, while not positively hostile, were as a rule unfriendly. An insolent stare was characteristic of most of them. Some disagreeable criticisms were pronounced, but Ah Cum's expression never changed, and we, of course, could not understand them. Once a banana-skin, thrown probably by a mischievous boy, flew by my head; and I was told that China's

A WHEELBARROW FOR FREIGHT.

favorite exclamation, "foreign devils," was often heard. But I dare say that if a Chinese mandarin, in full regalia, were to walk through some of our streets, he would not fare as well as we did in Canton; and that if he ever went to the Bowery, "he'd never go there any more."

ONE OF THE BROADEST STREETS.

As we kept passing on through other alleys teeming with half-clad specimens of the great unwashed, I called to mind the fact that this low class in China has been deliberately taught to hate, despise, and thoroughly distrust all foreigners. The unjust opium war with England, the recent territorial war with France, the stories told them of the treatment of their countrymen in the United States,—all these would, of

CHINESE TEA-PICKERS.

themselves, be enough to make them hostile; but they are as nothing to the effect produced upon an ignorant, superstitious populace by the placards posted on the walls of many Chinese cities. I read translations of a few of these, and I believe they cannot be surpassed in literature for the vulgarity and infamy of their accusations. They are in one sense perfectly absurd; but when we recollect the riotous acts to which they

CHINESE MERCHANTS DRINKING TEA.

have frequently incited their deluded victims, they challenge serious consideration.

On entering some of the shops that line these passageways, I was astonished at the contrast they presented to the streets themselves. The latter are at times no more than four feet wide. Not so the shops. Many of them have a depth of eighty feet, and in the centre are entirely open to the roof. In the corner of each is placed a little shrine. A gallery extends around the second story, and on that floor, or in the rear of the building, the owners live. Some of these shops are handsomely adorned with fine wood-carving and bronze lamps, and on the shelves is stored a great variety of goods, frequently including articles as dissimilar as silk and cotton fabrics, fans, jewelry, umbrellas, Waterbury clocks, and Chinese shoes.

HALL IN A CHINESE HOUSE.

Among these shops we saw a building used partly as a temple and partly as the Guild Hall for the Canton silk merchants. Guilds, or trade-unions, have existed here for centuries. They permeate every branch of Chinese industry, legal and illegal. Even the thieves form themselves into a guild, and I suppose there is "honor" among them. The origin of these unions is partly due to unjust taxation. Canton contains a vast amount of wealth, but those possessing it are careful to conceal all trace of any superabundance. On this account disputes between the various guilds are settled by arbitra-

A CHINESE BED AND FURNITURE.

tion. To allow their affairs to go into court would show too plainly to the tax-collectors their financial status. Accordingly litigation is almost unknown. Moreover, when a case is settled by arbitration, the losing party not only pays the disputed sum, but is obliged to give a supper to the victor.

In another building that we passed I saw a curious ceremony, which Ah Cum explained as that of three Buddhist priests who were clearing a house of evil spirits. It appears that, two weeks before, a man had committed suicide on the premises, in order to avenge himself on the proprietor. For in China a man, instead of killing his enemy, sometimes kills himself, the motive being a desire that the hated one shall be regarded as responsible for his death, and be pursued by evil spirits here and in the world to come. To be annoyed by ghosts must be exceedingly unpleasant, but, on the whole, I hope that all my enemies will try the Chinese method.

EXORCISING SPIRITS.

Occasionally we discovered in these streets an itinerant barber. These Chinese Figaros carry their outfits with them. First in importance comes a bamboo pole, which is the immemorial badge of their profession. To this is usually attached one solitary towel,—free to every customer. From one extremity of this pole hangs a small brass basin, together with a charcoal stove for heating water; the other end is balanced by a wooden cabinet, which serves the patient as a

LADY AND MAID.

seat during the operation, and contains razors, lancets, tweezers, files, and other surgical instruments.

It matters not where one of these tonsorial artists practises his surgery. A temple court, a flight of steps, a street, or a back-yard, are quite the same to him. He takes his queue where he can find it. One of his commonest duties is to braid that customary appendage to a Chinaman's head, without which he would be despised. It is comical to estimate the thousands of miles of Chinese queues which even one barber twists in the course of his career—enough, if tied together, end to end, to form a cable between Europe and America. Yet this singular style of hair-dressing (now so universal) was introduced into China only two hundred and fifty years ago. Before that time the Chinese, wore full heads of hair, and the present fashion of shaved crowns and twisted queues is of Tartar origin, and was imposed by a conquering dynasty as a badge of servitude. The wearing of a mustache in China is an indication that he whose face it adorns is a grandfather. In fact, until he is forty-five years old, a Chinaman usually shaves his face completely; but this fact does not prove that after that time he can dispense with the services of a barber. For the tonsorial art in China is exceedingly varied; and Chinese barbers not

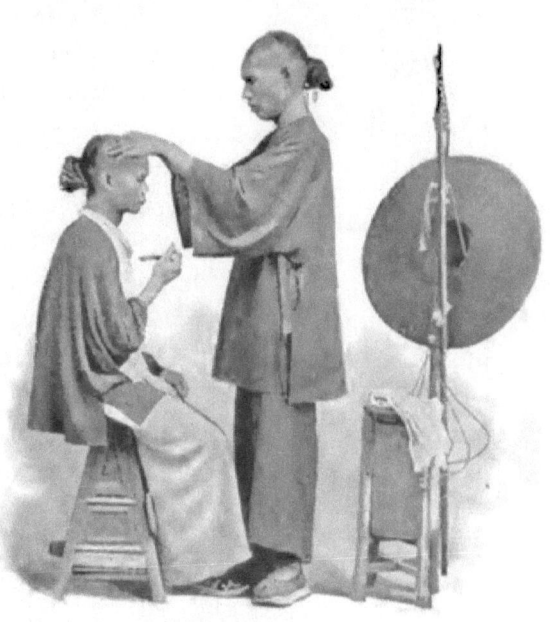

CHINESE BARBER.

A CHINESE MERCHANT.

only braid the queue; they also shave the eyebrows, clean the ears, pull teeth, and massage. Moreover, they scrape the inside of their victim's eyelids — a custom which is believed by foreigners to be the cause of much of the ophthalmia in China.

Chinese fortune-tellers had for me a singular fascination. I found them everywhere — in temple courts, at gateways and beside the roads — invariably wearing spectacles, and usually seated at a table decorated with huge Chinese characters. Their services seemed to be in great demand. In every case the ceremony was the same. Each applicant in turn approached, and stated what he wished to know; for example, whether a certain day would be a lucky time for him to buy some real estate, or which of several girls his son would better marry. Upon the table stood a tin box full of bamboo sticks. One of these slips the customer drew at random, and from the sentence written on it the fortune-teller gave his answer in oracular words — which could, as usual, be interpreted in various ways.

A CHINESE FORTUNE-TELLER.

A WALL OF CANTON.

At length, however, leaving for a time the shops and dimly-lighted alleys, we found ourselves approaching a huge gate. For Canton, like most other Chinese cities, is divided into certain districts, each of which is separated from the adjoining one by a wall. The gateways in these walls are always closed at night, and are of special use in case of fires or insurrections, since they are strong enough to hold in check a surging crowd till the police or soldiers can arrive.

Passing through this portal, we made our way along the wall until we arrived at a prominent point of observation, known as the Five-storied Pagoda. Whatever this may once have been, it is to-day a shabby, barn-like structure, marked here and there with traces of red paint, like daubs of rouge on a clown's face. All visitors to Canton, however, will recollect the building, with a certain amount of pleasure, as being the resting-place

THE FIVE-STORIED PAGODA.

in which one eats the lunch brought from the steamer or hotel. Not that there is not food of certain kinds obtainable in Canton itself, but somehow what one sees of Chinese delicacies here does not inspire him with a desire to partake of

A WAYSIDE RESTAURANT.

them. In one of Canton's streets, for example, I entered a cat-restaurant. Before the door was a notice which Ah Cum translated thus: "Two fine black cats to-day, ready soon." On stepping inside, I heard some pussies mewing piteously in bamboo cages. Hardly had I entered when a poor old woman brought the proprietor some kittens for sale. He felt of them to test their plumpness, as we might weigh spring chickens. Only a small price was offered, as they were very thin, but the bargain was soon concluded, the woman took her money, and the cadaverous kittens went to swell the chorus in the cages. Black cats, by the way, cost more in China than cats of any other color, for the Chinese believe that the flesh of dark-coated felines makes good blood.

To some Chinamen, dogs fried in oil are also irresistible. In one untidy street, swarming with yellow-skinned humanity, we saw a kind of gipsy kettle hung over a wood fire. Within it was a stew of dog-meat. Upon a pole close by was hung a rump of uncooked dog, with the tail left on, to show the patrons of this open-air restaurant to what particular breed the animal had belonged. For it is said there is a great difference in the flesh of dogs. Bull-terriers, for example, would probably be considered tough. Around this kettle stood a group of coolies, each with a plate and spoon, devouring the canine stew as eagerly as travelers eat sandwiches at a railway restaurant after the warning bell has rung. Some hungry ones were looking on as wistfully as boys outside a bun-shop. One man had such a famished look that, through the medium of Ah Cum, I treated him at once. Moreover, hundreds of rats, dried and hung up by the tails, are exposed for sale in Canton streets, and shark's fins, antique duck eggs, and sea-slugs are considered delicacies.

We tried to bring back photographic proofs of all these horrors, but it was impossible. Whenever we halted in the

CHINAMEN OUT ON A PICNIC.

narrow lanes, in fifteen seconds we would be encircled by a moving wall of hideous faces, whose foremost rank kept closing in on us until the atmosphere grew so oppressive that we gasped for breath and told our bearers to move on. Nor is this all. These crowds were sometimes positively hostile. A superstitious fear of being photographed by "foreign devils" made them dangerous. This fact was several times made dis-

THE SACRED HOGS.

agreeably evident. Thus, in a garden adjoining a Chinese temple, I wished to photograph some "sacred" hogs which were attached to the sanctuary in some unknown capacity. But scarcely had the exposure been made, when a priest gave the alarm, and in three minutes a mob of men and boys were rushing toward us, uttering yells and throwing

SORTING TEA.

stones. Ah Cum himself turned pale. He sprang in front of us, and swore (may heaven forgive him!) that not a picture had been taken. Of course we offered money as indemnity, but

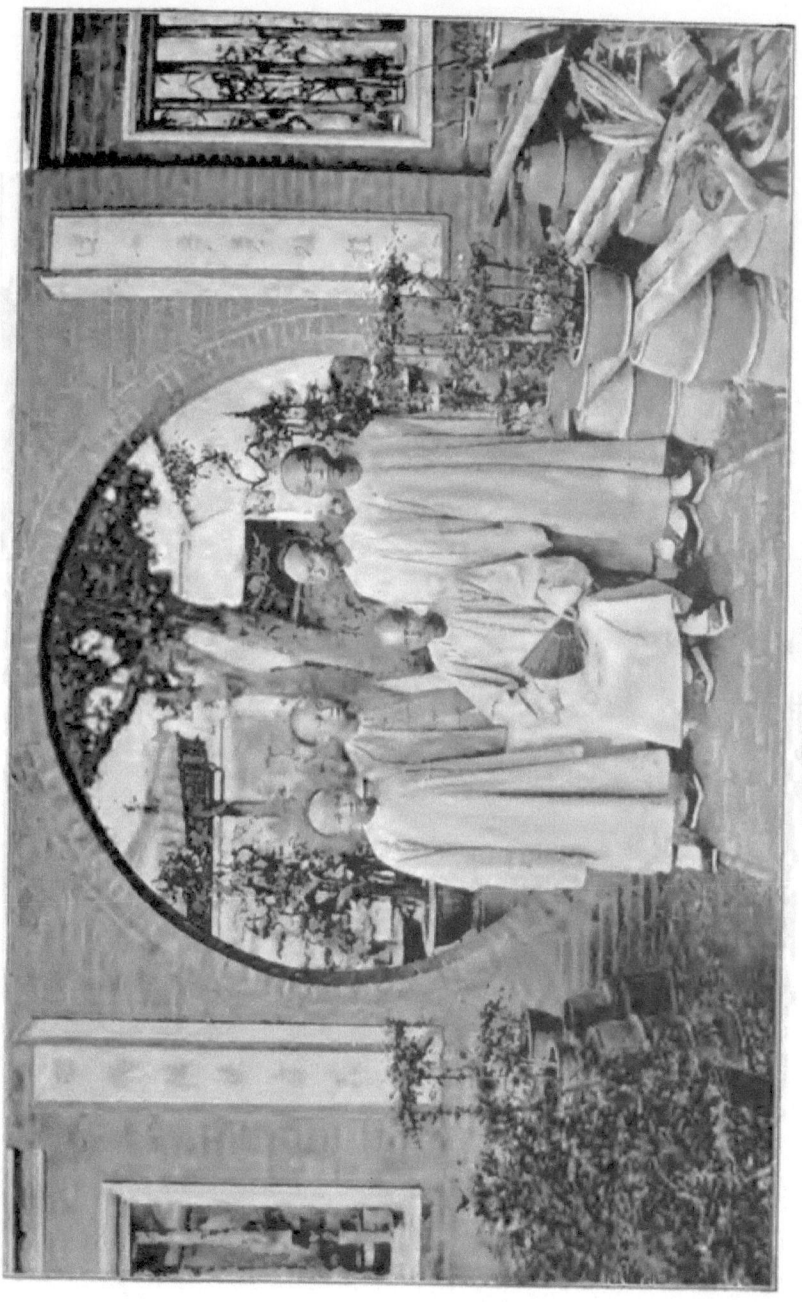

CHINESE MERCHANTS

the priests rejected it with scorn, claiming that by the pointing of the camera we had stopped the growth of the hogs. I do not think I exaggerate the situation when I say that if the politic Ah Cum had not been there to defend us, we should have suffered personal injury.

A CHINESE FARM-HOUSE.

Standing upon the summit of the Five-storied Pagoda, we looked out over the city of Canton. For widespread, unrelieved monotony, I never saw the equal of that view in any place inhabited by human beings. True, the confusion of the foreground was to be excused, since a tornado had recently blown down many of the native houses. But far beyond this mass of ruins, stretching on and on for miles, was the same monotonous, commonplace vista of low, uninteresting buildings, seamed with mere crevices in lieu of streets. Meantime, from this vast area came to us a dull, persistent hum, like the escape of steam from a locomotive, reminding us that here were swarming nearly two million human beings, almost as difficult for a foreigner to distinguish or identify as ants in a gigantic ant-hill.

THE FLOWERY PAGODA, CANTON.

The exact population of Canton is hard to determine. The number arrived at depends upon where one leaves off counting the three hundred suburban villages, each of which seems a part of the city. Bishop Harper, who lived here for forty years, says, that if one should plant a stake in the centre of Canton, and count all around it within a radius of ten miles, one would find an aggregate of three-and-a-half million people. One village, for example, eleven miles away, noted for silk and other manufactures, is thought to contain eight hundred thousand inhabitants.

CANTONESE PAWN-SHOPS.

Out of this wilderness of mediocrity there rose in one place a pagoda, which by contrast seemed to possess prodigious height; but such objects are exceptional. To understand what Canton is like, one must picture to himself a city which, with its suburbs, is larger and more populous than Paris, yet has not one handsome avenue, one spacious square, or even one street that possesses the slightest claim to cleanliness or beauty. Worse than this, it is a city without a single Chinese building in its whole extent that can be even distantly compared in architectural elegance with thousands of imposing structures in any other city of the civilized world. "But are there no European edifices in Canton?" the reader may perhaps inquire. Yes, one, which makes the contrast only more apparent. It is the Roman Catholic cathedral, whose lofty towers are, strangely enough, the first objects in the city which the traveler sees in sailing up the river from Hong-Kong. This handsome Gothic structure, built entirely of granite, rising from such a sea of architectural ugliness, at once called forth our admiration. To the Chinese, however, these graceful towers are objects of the utmost hatred. It angers them to see this area, which French and English conquerors obtained by treaty, still occupied by a Christian church. So far, it has escaped destruction; but there are those who prophesy its doom and say that the time will come when not one stone of it will be left upon another.

There are, however, five or six other buildings in Canton, which rival the pagoda and the Catholic church in height. These hideous objects, which look like monstrous granite boxes set on end, are pawn-shops. One might conclude from their enormous size that half the personal property of the Cantonese was in pawn. They certainly are well patronized, for pawning clothes is such a common thing in China that hundreds of the

CATHOLIC CATHEDRAL, CANTON.

Cantonese send here for safe-keeping their furs and overcoats in summer, and their thin summer clothes in winter, receiving money for them as from any pawn-broker. The Chinese mode of guarding these tall structures against thieves is certainly unique. Upon the roofs are piled stones to be dropped upon the heads of robbers, and also reservoirs of vitriol, with syringes to squirt the horrible acid on invaders.

Astonished at this lack of imposing architecture, we asked

TEMPLE OF FIVE HUNDRED GODS.

if there were no temples in Canton. Assuredly there were— eight hundred of them, all more or less defaced and incrusted with dirt. One of the oldest and most sacred is called the "Temple of Five Hundred Gods," because within its walls are seated five hundred life-size images of gilded wood, representing deified sages of the Buddhist faith. But they are all coarse specimens of sculpture, and many are amusing caricatures. In front of each is a small jar of ashes, in which the worshiper burns a stick of incense in honor of his favorite god. Offerings of money, too, are sometimes made—but not of genuine money. The Chinese are usually too practical to use anything but imitation money made of gilded paper. I do not know what the gods think of this Oriental style

AN OLD TEMPLE, CANTON.

of dropping buttons in the contribution-box, but the priests do not like this sort of currency. They are all "hard money" men.

But, if we accept the ancient proverb that "To labor is to pray," then are the Chinese devout indeed. Whatever other faults they may possess, idleness is not one of them. The struggle for existence keeps them active. Yet they live on almost nothing. A German merchant told me that one

APPROACH TO A SHRINE.

of his coolies, after twenty-five years of service, had recently had his salary raised to ten dollars a month. The laborer was, of course, delighted. "Now," he exclaimed, "I intend to marry another wife. For years I have longed to have two wives, but have never been able to afford it; but now, with ten dollars a month, I can indulge in luxuries!"

In strolling about among these Chinese coolies, I found that life in China is indeed reduced to its lowest terms. In some of the Canton shops, for example, I saw potatoes sold in halves and even in quarters, and poultry is offered, not only singly, but by the piece—so much for a leg, so much for a wing. Second-hand nails are sold in lots of half-a-dozen. A man can buy one-tenth of a cent's worth of fish or rice. I understood, at last, how Chinese laundrymen can go home from the United States after a few years' work, and live upon their incomes. When one perceives under what conditions these swarming myriads live, one naturally asks how pestilence can be averted.

ONE OF THE MANY.

One source of safety is, no doubt, the universal custom of drinking only boiled water in the form of tea. If it were not for this, there would be inevitably a terrible mortality, for the coolies take no precautions against infection. A gentleman in the English consular service told us that he had seen two Canton women in adjoining boats, one washing in the river the bedclothes of her husband who had died of cholera, the other dipping up water in which to cook the family dinner!

If, perchance, these people should fall ill, I fear they would not be greatly benefited by any Chinese doctor whom they might employ. Chinese physicians are thought to be ignoramuses, unless they can diagnose a case by merely feeling the pulse. Hence, if they are called to attend a lady, they see of her usually nothing but her wrist, thrust out between the curtains of the bed. Those who prescribe for internal diseases are called "inside doctors," while others are "outside" men, just as some of our medicines are labeled "for external use only." A story is told of a man who had been shot through the arm with an arrow. He first applied to an "outside" doctor, who cut off the two ends of the weapon and put a plaster on each wound. "But," said the patient, "the remainder of the arrow is still in my arm." "Ah!" replied the "outside" doctor, "that is not my affair. To have that removed, you must go to an 'inside' man."

One day, in passing through a temple gate, a half-clad Chinaman offered me for sale a box of grasshoppers, which, when ground into a powder, make a popular remedy for some ailments. In fact,

A CHINESE DOCTOR.

aside from ginseng and a few other well-known herbs, the medicines used in China seem almost incredible. A favorite cure for fever, for example, is a soup of scorpions. Dysentery is treated by running a needle through the tongue. The flesh of rats is supposed to make the hair grow. Dried lizards are recommended as a tonic for "that tired feeling," and

A MEMORIAL GATE.

iron filings are said to be a good astringent. Chinese physicians say that certain diseases are curable only by a decoction whose chief ingredient is a piece of flesh cut from the arm or thigh of the patient's son or daughter. To supply this flesh is thought to be one of the noblest proofs of filial devotion. This is not an exaggeration. In the Pekin *Official Gazette* of July 5, 1870, is an editorial, calling the emperor's attention to a young girl who had cut off two joints of her finger and dropped them into her mother's medicine. The mother recovered, and the governor of the province proposed to erect a monument in honor of the child.

In view of such a pharmacopœia, it is a comfort to learn that in the Chinese theology a

BEGGARS ON THE TEMPLE STEPS.

A CHINESE FUNERAL PROCESSION.

special place in hell is assigned to ignorant physicians. All quacks are doomed to centuries of torture, the worst fate being reserved for doctors who abuse their professional skill for purposes of immorality. Their punishment is the cheerful one of being boiled in oil. Another curious, and not altogether absurd, custom of the Chinese is to pay a physician so long as they continue in health, but if they fall ill, the

A GROUP OF CHINESE WOMEN.

doctor's salary ceases until they recover, whereupon it commences again.

Chinese women seemed to me, as a rule, exceedingly plain, but, even were they Venuses, one of their characteristics would make my flesh creep. I refer to their claw-like finger-nails, which are so long that apparently they could be used with equal ease as paper-cutters or stilettoes. Gloves cannot possibly be worn upon these finger-spikes, so metal sheaths have been invented to protect them. To show what

LILY FEET.

can be done in nail-growing, the following lengths were measured on the left hand of a Chinese belle: thumb nail, two inches; little finger nail, four inches; third finger, five and one-quarter inches. Under these circumstances we cannot wonder that in China it is not the custom to shake hands: otherwise, painful accidents might occur. Accordingly, the Chinese clasp their own hands and shake them gently at each other.

A still more repulsive peculiarity of Chinese women is their stunted feet, which for the purposes of locomotion are little better than hoofs. All Chinese ladies of the better class must have these "lily feet," as they are called. Sometimes a Chinaman will have two wives; the first an ornamental one with "lily feet," the second, a large-footed woman for business. The origin of this barbarous custom of preventing the growth of the foot is unknown. Perhaps it sprang from a sentiment which Ah Cum graphically expressed by saying: "A small foot is much safer to live with. A big foot runs about too easily and gets into mischief. Moreover," he added, with a

MOTHER AND CHILD.

smile, "a big-footed woman sometimes kicks." One Chinaman assured me with great pride that his wife's foot was only two and a half inches long. There is a class of women here whose regular business it is to bind the feet of little girls when about six years of age. The process of repressing the natural growth of the foot lasts for seven years—the four smaller toes being bent under until they lose their articulations and become identified with the sole of the foot. When this has been accomplished, the second and severer operation commences— of bringing the great toe and the heel as nearly together as possible. The bandage is drawn tighter, month by month, until the base of the great toe is brought into contact with the heel, and the foot has become a shapeless lump. By this unnatural treatment the leg itself becomes deformed, and its bones are made not only smaller in diameter, but shorter. The circulation also is obstructed, and the large muscles are soon completely atrophied from disuse. The agony caused by such interference with nature can be only faintly imagined. It made the tears come to my eyes to hear a Chinese gentleman describe the methods taken to console his suffering children and help them forget their misery. The poor little creatures scream and moan from the incessant pain, and often lie across the bed

A DISTORTED FOOT.

with their legs pressed against the edge, in the hope that this will lessen their distress; but nothing can relieve them but freedom from the torturing bandage, which is never relaxed. It makes one sick at heart to think that such a custom has prevailed in China for more than a thousand years.

Should we approach a group of Chinese merchants in Canton, and ask any one of them "How many children have you?" we could be almost certain that he would not think of counting his daughters, or that he would at least make this distinction—"I have two children, and one girl." For to a Chinaman nothing in life is so important as to have a son to offer sacrifices for him after death and worship at his grave, since, in their opinion, a daughter is not capable of doing this. When a boy is born, therefore, the father is overwhelmed with congratulations, but if the newcomer be a girl, as little reference as possible is made to the misfortune. Friends are informed of the birth of a child by strips of paper carried through the street. If it be a boy, yellow paper is used, but in case of a girl any color will do. This feeling, intensified by poverty, is the cause of the infanticide which has been, and still is, in certain provinces, so dark a blot on the domestic history of China. It is said, for example, that in the vicinity of Amoy thirty per cent. of all new-born girls are strangled or drowned, as unwelcome kittens sometimes are with us.

A CHINESE LADY.

On our second day in Canton we investigated another

phase of Chinese life, in some respects stranger than anything we had thus far seen. Along the shores of the Canton river, and in its various canals, is a population of a quarter of a million souls,

THE HOMES OF THOUSANDS.

living on thousands of peculiar boats crowded together side by side, and forming streets, and even colonies, of floating dwellings. Moreover, these conditions prevail in every river-town throughout the empire.

Each of these "sampans," as they are called, though only about twenty feet in length, constitutes the home of an entire family. Eight people frequently live on one boat—grandpa and grandma, father and mother, uncle and aunt, two or three children, and a baby. The latter is tied to the back of its mother, even when she is rowing. As for the other children, their parents fasten around them pieces of bamboo, like life-preservers, and tie them to the rail

A CHINESE PATERFAMILIAS.

by a cord. If they tumble over, they float until some one gets a chance to pull them in. Upon these little boats thousands are born, eat, drink, cook, and sleep, and finally die, having known no other home. Under the flooring are stored their cooking utensils, bedding, clothing, provisions, oil, charcoal, and other requisites of their aquatic life. Above them,

A MARKET-PLACE.

usually, are movable roofs of bamboo wicker-work, to give protection from the sun and rain.

Some of these families even take boarders! I verified this by going at night among this floating population, and found that sleeping space on the boats is rented to those who have no fixed abode. Planks are laid over the seats to form a floor, and on these lie the numerous members of the household and

CHINA

the lodgers. Conspicuous figures in this boat-life are the itinerant barbers and physicians, who go about in tiny *sampans*, ringing a bell and offering their services.

Occasionally, however, we beheld a boat much larger and finer than the craft around it. It proved to be one of the Chinese flower-boats, which are the pleasure resorts of China's *jeunesse dorée*. By day they are conspicuous by their size and gilded wood-work, and in the evening by their many lights. Never, while memory lasts, shall I forget an excursion made at night with our hotel-proprietor among these flower-boats and their surroundings. Many of them were anchored side by side, and planks were stretched from one to the other, like a continuous sidewalk. As we walked along, we passed by countless open doors, each of which revealed a room handsomely furnished with mirrors, marble panels, and blackwood furniture. Here were usually grouped a dozen or more hilarious Chinamen, who were eating, drinking, and smoking, together with professional singing-girls, who are hired by the owners of these flower-boats to entertain their guests with songs and dances. We could not pause to observe them care-

A FLOWER-BOAT.

fully, for foreigners are not wanted here, either as visitors or patrons. Meanwhile, at the very doorways of these handsome rooms, beggars in greasy garments crowded around us and almost threateningly demanded alms. "Look out for your pockets," was the proprietor's constant warning.

I have an indistinct remembrance of thus passing row after row of lighted boats, room after room of painted girls, group after group of sleek, fat Chinamen at tables, and then, on leaving these, of seeing miles of loathsome boats contain-

CHINESE MUSICIANS.

ing half-clad men stretched out on bunks and stupefied by opium, hag-like females cooking over charcoal braziers, and ragged children huddled in dark corners. I have a vivid recollection, too, of walking over slimy planks, of breathing pestilential odors, and of looking down on patches of repulsive water, so thick with refuse that they resembled in the lamp-light tanks of cabbage-soup. We also shudderingly passed some leper-boats, whose inmates are afflicted with that terrible disease, and who are forced to live as outcasts, begging for alms by holding out a little bag suspended from a bamboo pole. But finally shaking off the beggars who had followed us, and fleeing from this multitudinous life, as one might turn with horror from a pool of wriggling eels, I staggered into the boat belonging to the hotel. As it moved out into clearer water, I drew a long breath and looked up at the stars. There they were—calm and glorious as ever—scattered in countless numbers through measureless space. At any time, when one looks off into the vault of night, our little globe seems insignificant, but never did it seem to me so tiny and comparatively valueless, as when I left these myriads of Chinamen, swarming like insects in their narrow boats, apparently the reduction of humanity to the grade of microbes.

A TYPICAL CHINESE CRAFT.

The gentleman who had accompanied me on this occasion was a Wall street broker. "Well," he exclaimed at last, "I have spent fifteen years among the Bulls and Bears, and I think my nerves are pretty strong, but for experiences which unnerve a man, and things which (glad as I am to have seen them once) I never wish to see again, nothing can compare with the sights and smells discovered in a trip to Chinatown!"

What impressed me most, however, in this experience was the idea that the millions in and around Canton are but an insignificant fraction of the Chinese race. It filled me with horror to reflect that all I had witnessed here was but a tiny sample of the entire empire. For Canton is said to be superior to many Chinese cities.

One writer has declared that, after walking through the Chinese quarter of Shanghai, he wanted to be hung on a clothes-line for a week in a gale of wind. Tientsin is said to be still worse for dirt and noxious odors. Even Pekin, from all accounts, has horribly paved and filthy thoroughfares, and its sanitary conditions are almost beyond belief. If such

A WHEELBARROW BUILT FOR TWO.

then be the state of things in the capital, what must it be in the interior towns, so rarely reached by foreigners?

It may, however, be objected that in the open ports, where they encounter foreign influence, the people are at their worst. But Chinamen are not impressionable, like the North American Indians or the aborigines on the islands in the Pacific, who eagerly adopt the vices of their conquerors, and speedily succumb to them.

China is one of the oldest countries in the world. Most of her ideas, customs, as well as the personal habits of her people are of immemorial antiquity, and her inhabitants are too conservative to change them. What one beholds in Canton, therefore, may be fairly supposed to exist from one extremity of the empire to the other.

But now, among so much that is disagreeable, one naturally inquires, "Are there not some redeeming features in this Chinese life?" I must confess there are not many discernible to the passing traveler, but I will gladly mention one about which I made careful inquiry. It is their honesty in business. It is the almost invariable custom for Chinese merchants every New-Year's day to settle their accounts, so that no errors may be carried over into the coming year; and I was told that if a tradesman fails to meet his liabilities at that time, he is considered a defaulter and his credit is forever lost. English and German merchants spoke to us of Chinese commercial honor in the highest terms, and drew comparisons in this respect between them and the Japanese which were not flattering to the latter.

Even in Japan, I found at all the foreign banks, in some of the shops, and in the Grand Hotel, that the cashiers were not Japanese, but Chinamen. Of course, one who has never traded with them cannot judge of their comparative abilities in a business way, but merchants in Yokohama, Shanghai, and Hong-Kong, as well as on the island of Shameen, told us that Chinamen were more trustworthy than the Japanese, and could be usually depended on to

A MARRIAGE PROCESSION.

live up to their contracts, whether they proved favorable or unfavorable.

An English gentleman who had resided both in China and Japan for years, once said to me: "The more you see of the Japanese the less you will like them. The more you see of the Chinese the less you will dislike them. You will always like the Japanese; you will always dislike Chinamen; but the degree in which you cherish and express these sentiments will constantly diminish."

A CHINESE JUNK.

Besides the numerous differences between Oriental and Occidental customs noticed in Japan, we found in China many other proofs of what has been well called a state of topsy-turvydom. Thus, our tailors draw the needle inward; Chinese tailors stitch outward. With us military men wear their swords on the left side; in China they are worn on the right. In boxing the compass a Chinaman says "East, West, South, North." To mark a place in a book we turn the corner of a page inside; a Chinaman bends it the other way. We print the title of a volume on the back; the Chinese on the front. We play battledore and shuttlecock with our hands; the Chinese use their feet for a battledore and catch the shuttlecock on their foreheads. We use our own names when engaged in business; in China fancy names are taken. We carry one watch hidden in our pocket; a Chinese gentleman sometimes wears two outside his clothes, with their faces exposed. We black our boots; the Chinese whiten theirs. With us it is considered impolite to ask a person's age; in China it is a high compliment, and there a man is congratulated if he

SACRED ROCKS, INTERIOR OF CHINA.

is old. Men, at least in the Occident, have plenty of pockets; the Chinaman has none, and uses his stockings as receptacles

LI HUNG CHANG'S VISITING-CARD.

for papers, and at the back of his neck inserts his folded fan. At our weddings youthful bridesmaids are desired; at Chinese nuptials old women serve in that capacity. We launch our vessels lengthwise; the Chinese launch theirs sidewise. We mount a horse from the left; they mount their horses from the right. We begin dinner with soup and fish, and end with dessert; they do exactly the reverse. Finally, the spoken language of China is never written, and the written language is never spoken.

After all, however, we should remember that Chinamen who travel in our own country think that our customs are as strange as theirs appear to us. A prominent official of the Flowery Kingdom, who made the tour of Europe several years ago, took notes of what he saw, and published them on his return. Among them are the following: "Women, when going to the drawing-room of Queen Victoria regard a bare skin as a mark of respect." "When people meet and wish to show affection, they put their lips and chins together and

A JOSS-HOUSE.

make a smacking sound." This is not so difficult to understand, when we recollect that, like most Orientals, the Chinese do not kiss, and that even a mother does not kiss her own baby, although she will press it to her cheek. Again, he thus describes our dancing parties: "A European skipping match is a strange sight. To this a number of men and women come in couples, and enter a spacious hall; there, at the sound of music, they grasp each other by both arms, and leap and prance backward and forward, and round and round,

WATERING-PLACE FOR ANIMALS.

till they are forced to stop for want of breath. All this," he adds, "is most extraordinary;" and when we Occidentals think of it, perhaps it is. A Chinese youth, after eating for the first time a European dinner, wrote of his experience: "Dishes of half-raw meat were served, from which pieces were cut with sword-like instruments and placed before the guests. Finally came a green and white substance, the smell of which was overpowering. This, I was informed, was a compound

PLACE OF EXECUTION, CANTON.

of sour milk, baked in the sun, under whose influence it remains until it becomes filled with insects; yet the greener and livelier it is, the greater the relish with which it is eaten! This is called *Che-sze*."

The object of most gruesome interest to me in Canton was its place of execution. On entering this, I looked about me with astonishment; for almost all the space between the rough brick walls was filled with coarse, cheap articles of pottery. Ah Cum explained, however, that when a batch of heads are to be cut off, the jars are all removed, much as a hotel

A PAGODA.

dining-room is cleared for dancing. The condemned prisoners are always brought in baskets to this place, and are compelled to kneel down with their hands tied behind their backs. Their queues are then thrown forward, and they are beheaded at a single stroke. Traces of blood were visible on the ground, and from a mass of rubbish close at hand a grinning Chinaman pulled out several skulls which he had hidden there, and claimed a fee for exhibiting them. I was presented to the executioner, and asked him how many men he had himself decapitated, but he could not tell. He kept no count, he said—some days six, some days ten, in all probably more than a thousand. As he was resolutely opposed to having his picture taken, we placed his two-edged sword against the wall, and photographed that. When I was told that, once a week, twenty or thirty men are brought into this filthy court to die like cattle in a slaughterhouse, I stood aghast, but when I subsequently learned that this is the only execution-place in a great province with a population of twenty

DRAWING WATER.

FEMALE CULPRITS.

millions, the number did not seem so appallingly excessive. This is, however, merely the average in ordinary times. After certain insurrections, such as the Taiping rebellion, this hideous square has seemed almost a reservoir of human blood. The venerable missionary, Dr. Williams, states that he saw here one morning at least two hundred headless trunks, and stacks of human heads piled six feet high. Careful estimates place the number executed here during fourteen months, at eighty-one thousand,— or more than thirteen hundred every week!

I doubt if many criminals beheaded here feel much regret at leaving life, so horrible has been their previous condition in the Canton prison. We visited this institution, but to obtain a picture of it was impossible. Within an ill-kept, loathsome area, we saw a crowd of prisoners wearing chains, while around their necks were heavy wooden collars, which, being from three to five

A PRISONER.

feet square, were so wide that the poor wretches wearing them could never possibly feed themselves, but must depend on others for their nourishment. How they lie down to sleep with them on I do not know. Yet they must wear such collars

JUDGE AND PRISONERS.

for weeks, and even months, at a time. I have no sentimental sympathy for criminals, and thoroughly believe in the enforcement of just laws, but I was shocked at the sight of these poor creatures. Whatever may have been their guilt, such treatment is a degradation of humanity.

Leaving the place of execution, we made our way to one of the criminal courts of Canton. It was in session when we entered it, and I never can forget the sight that met my gaze. Before the judge was a prisoner on his knees, pleading for mercy and protesting innocence. Chains were around his neck, waist, wrists, and ankles. Beside him knelt an aged woman, whose gray hair swept the floor as she rocked back and forth, imploring vengeance on her son's assassin. At last the culprit confessed his crime of murder, and was led back to prison. How sincere his confession was, it would be hard to say; for if, in the face of powerful adverse testimony, an accused man still asserts his innocence, he is often punished in the court-room till he does confess. Around the hall were various instruments of torture—bamboo rods to flog the naked back; hard leather straps with which to strike the prisoner on the mouth, thus sometimes breaking the teeth and even the jaw; thumb-screws and cords by which he is suspended by his thumbs and toes; and heavy sticks with which to beat his ankles. I did not happen to see these used, because in the three trials I witnessed all of the prisoners confessed. But they are used; and just as I was entering the court, I met a criminal being led back to prison, so weak and crippled by his punishment, that he could hardly step without assistance. Curiously enough, after the torture has been administered, the culprit is required to fall upon his knees and thank the judge. This I should think would be "the most unkindest cut of all."

It seems impossible to say anything in defense of such a system as this; for in China a man is not only looked upon as guilty till he is proved innocent, but is kept in loathsome confinement, and may be even put upon the rack, in spite of the established fact that torture is never a test of truth. And yet a foreign resident made, as an apology, the following statement: "You must re-

A CHINESE COURT.

member that testimony here amounts to nothing, and that, by paying sixpence apiece, you can pack the court-room with men who will swear that black is white. Hence, where a man can easily bribe false witnesses to ruin his enemy, the Chinese law provides that no one shall under any circumstances be put to death unless he has confessed his crime. But since a prisoner on trial for his life will usually protest his innocence to the last, the court attempts by torture to force him to confess."

We visited finally an object in Canton far pleasanter than its scenes of punishment, yet equally characteristic of the national life. It is the place where natives of this province take the first step in the only path which in China leads to political and social rank. It is the scene of the competitive examinations, the fame of which has filled the world.

THE EXAMINATION GROUND, CANTON.

The courtyard where the contest takes place is by no means inviting. It is an area of sixteen acres, covered with nearly nine thousand rough brick sheds. At the time of an examination each of these is occupied by a candidate. Before he enters it, his person is carefully searched, and soldiers and policemen guard all passageways to prevent communication. "Each in his narrow cell," these applicants for office then remain for three consecutive days and nights, about as pleasantly lodged, I should imagine, as Jonah was for the same length of time; for these dirty dens of brick are only four feet long, three feet wide, and possibly six feet high. One of the horse-sheds in the rear of a New England meeting-

THE GREAT WALL AT A PRECIPICE.

house would be a far more comfortable place in which to eat and sleep. Perhaps they are meant, however, to emphasize the triumph of mind over matter. Their only furniture consists of two small planks, one for a seat, the other for a table. Rest is, of course, impossible in such a cage, and candidates have sometimes died here from physical and mental strain. All this seems inexcusably cruel; yet the Chinese government may have good reasons for maintaining this severity. For instance, such a system, if introduced at Washington, would rid the District of Columbia of nine-tenths of its office-seekers within twenty-four hours. While some of these students persevere in their attempts till they are seventy or eighty years of age, others are quite young; but the fact of youth is not considered discreditable, for Confucius said: "A youth should always be regarded with respect. How do we know that his future may not be superior to our present?" At all events, the highest place is open to them, if their brains will take them there; for every village in China has its school, and every freeborn citizen may qualify for this struggle, the governing principle of

A STUDENT.

FISHING ON THE RIVER.

which is "Let the best man win!" It is the law of the "survival of the fittest" exemplified in politics.

In all the provinces of China, on the appointed day, thousands of candidates assemble, eager for the contest. Subjects are given them on which they must produce a poem and original essays. Their work is then examined by officials ap-

A CHINESE GENERAL AND HIS ATTENDANTS.

pointed by the Government, and so extremely rigid is the test, that out of every thousand applicants only about ten gain the first, or "District," degree. There are, however, three degrees to be attained by Chinese aspirants for fame. Those who come out as victors in the first receive no office, but are at least exempt from corporal punishment, and may attempt the examination for the next degree. Even the few who pass the second, or "Provincial," test (about one in a hundred) receive no government appointment. Yet they are distinguished among their countrymen by wearing a gold button in their hats, and by a sign over their houses signifying "Promoted man."

Those who succeed in standing the third, or "Imperial," test at Pekin,—severer even than the other two,—have reached the apex of the pyramid. They are now mandarins, and have acquired all they can desire,— social distinction, office, wealth, and (what is sometimes still more highly prized) great national fame. For in the results of this examination the entire country takes the greatest interest. The names of the successful men are everywhere proclaimed by means of couriers, river-boats, and carrier-pigeons, since thousands of people in the empire have laid their wagers on the candidates, as we might do on horses at the Derby. Strange, is it not, to think that this elaborate Chinese system was practised in the land of the Mongols substantially as it is to-day, at a time when England was inhabited by painted savages?

LI HUNG CHANG.

Moreover, the honors of successful candidates in China cannot be inherited. Young men, if they would be ennobled, must surpass their competitors and win their places as their fathers did. Even the youthful son of Li Hung Chang, whom General Grant considered, next to Bismarck, the most remarkable man he met with in his tour around the world, is not entitled, because of his father's office, to any special rank. Hence, China, though an absolute monarchy, has no privileged class whose claims rest merely on the accident of birth. Her aristocracy consists of those who have repeatedly proved themselves intellectually superior to their rivals. Among no people in the world, therefore, have literary men received such honors as in China; and it is a remarkable fact that this vast nation has worshiped for two thousand years, not a great

LI HUNG CHANG AND SUITE ON THEIR TOUR AROUND THE WORLD.

warrior, nor even a prophet claiming inspiration from God, but a philosopher,—Confucius.

I have often thought that were I asked to compare the Chinese empire of to-day with some material object, I would select for such comparison the Great Wall on its northern frontier. This mighty work has hardly been surpassed in the whole history of architecture, not even by the builders of the Pyramids. It is no less than twenty-five feet high and forty feet broad, with watch-towers higher still, at intervals of three hundred feet. And yet it has a length of nearly fifteen hundred miles, a distance exceeding that from Boston to St. Paul, and in its uninterrupted march spans deep ravines and climbs to lofty mountain crests, in one place nearly five thousand feet in height. Although it was built three hundred years before the birth of Christ, it still exists, and during fourteen

THE GREAT WALL OF CHINA.

centuries sufficed to hold in check the savage tribes of Tartars from the north. It has been calculated that if the Great Wall were constructed at the present time, and with Caucasian labor, its cost would pay for all the railroads in the United States. One hundred years ago an English engineer reckoned that its masonry represented more than all the dwellings of England and Scotland put together, and, finally, that its material would construct a stone wall six feet high and two feet thick around the entire globe.

In many respects this great rampart is typical of China. Both have a vast antiquity, both have an enormous extent, and both have had their periods of glory, — China her age of progress and invention, and this old wall a time when it was kept in perfect order, when warriors stood at every tower, and when it stretched for fifteen hundred miles—an insurmountable barrier to invasion. But just as this leviathan of masonry has outlived its usefulness, and is at present crumbling to decay, so the huge Chinese empire itself now seems decrepit and wholly alien to the nineteenth century. Her roads, once finely kept, are now disgraceful; her streets are an abomination to the senses; her rivers and canals are left to choke themselves through want of dredging; and even her temples show few signs of care. Stagnation and neglect are steadily at work on her colossal frame, as weeds and plants disintegrate this mouldering wall. Will this old empire ever be aroused to new activity, and can fresh life-blood be infused into her shrunken veins to animate her inert frame? There is, I think, a possibility that, in the coming century, the new, progressive party here will overcome

A GATEWAY IN THE GREAT WALL.

the dull conservatism of the nation, connect her vast interior with the sea, utilize her mineral wealth, develop her immense resources, and make her one of the great powers of the world. Napoleon once warned England that if the Chinese should learn too well from her the art of war, and then acquire the thirst for conquest which has characterized other nations, the result might be appalling to the whole of Europe. For think what inexhaustible armies they could raise, and what great fleets they could build and launch upon their mighty rivers! But this is a problem of the future, about which no man can predict with certainty.

Many have asked me if I am glad that I went to China, and I have always answered that, as a unique and useful study of humanity, I think it one of the most valuable experiences of my life. Still I am bound to say, that when I stood upon the deck of an outgoing steamer, and felt it move beneath my feet responsive to the engine's stroke, I drew a breath of pleasure and relief. For I was assured that the

A LEVIATHAN OF MASONRY.

swarming millions of the Chinese empire were being left behind me, and that my face was turned toward that historic land where, lighted by the Southern Cross, I was to visit Hindu shrines and Mogul palaces, and gaze on the Himalayas and the Taj Mahal.

www.ingramcontent.com/pod-product-compliance
Lightning Source LLC
Chambersburg PA
CBHW020141170426
43199CB00010B/835